A Field of
Vision

By the same author

POEMS
Farewell, Aggie Weston
Survivor's Leave
Union Street
Johnny Alleluia
Underneath the Water
Figure of 8: Narrative Poems
Figgie Hobbin
Collected Poems 1951–1975
The Hill of the Fairy Calf
The Animals' Carol
Secret Destinations
Early in the Morning
Jack the Treacle Eater

VERSE PLAYS
The Gift of a Lamb
The Ballad of Aucassin and Nicolette

TRANSLATION
25 Poems by Hamdija Demirović

SHORT STORIES
Hands to Dance and Skylark

CHILDREN'S STORIES
The Tail of the Trinosaur
(in verse)
Dick Whittington
Three Heads Made of Gold
The Last King of Cornwall

AS EDITOR
Peninsula
Dawn and Dusk
Rising Early
Modern Folk Ballads
The Puffin Book of Magic Verse
The Puffin Book of Salt-Sea Verse
The Batsford Book of Story Poems
The Sun, Dancing

A Field of
Vision

Charles Causley

MACMILLAN
LONDON

Copyright © Charles Causley 1988

All rights reserved. No reproduction, copy or transmission
of this publication may be made without written permission.
No paragraph of this publication may be reproduced, copied
or transmitted save with written permission or in
accordance with the provisions of the Copyright Act 1956
(as amended). Any person who does any unauthorised act
in relation to this publication may be liable to criminal
prosecution and civil claims for damages.

First published 1988 by
MACMILLAN LONDON LIMITED
4 Little Essex Street London WC2R 3LF
and Basingstoke

Associated companies in Auckland, Delhi, Dublin, Gaborone,
Hamburg, Harare, Hong Kong, Johannesburg, Kuala Lumpur,
Lagos, Manzini, Melbourne, Mexico City, Nairobi, New York,
Singapore and Tokyo

British Library Cataloguing in Publication Data
Causley, Charles, 1917–
Fields of vision.
I. Title
821'.912

ISBN 0-333-48263-8

Typeset by Wyvern Typesetting Ltd, Bristol
Printed in Hong Kong

Contents

Acknowledgements ix

Boulge 1
Sibard's Well 2
Bridie Wiles 3
Dick Lander 5
Kelly Wood 7
This Clock 8
Sunday School Outing 10
Buffalo 12
Gelibolu 14
Seder 15
A Little Story 17
Bugis Street 18
In Malacca 20
Arshile Gorky's *The Artist and His Mother* 21
I believe you were born in Odessa 23
On the Eastern Front 25
A Song of Truth 26
In the Dome Car 28
A Tamarack Goose 30
At the Château Lake Louise 31
Myth 33

Samuel Palmer's *Coming from Evening Church* 36
St Godric and the Hart 37
The Prodigal Son 39
Legend of the Raven 40
Embryos 41
Letter to W.S. Graham 43
I love the laurel green 47
Calico 48
The Mystery of St Mylor 49
At St Hilary 51
St Protus & St Hyacinth, Blisland 52
Trethevy Quoit 53
Red 55
My Enemy 56
When I Was 14 58
Family Feeling 59
In 1933 61
Eden Rock 62

Note 63
Index of titles 65
Index of first lines 67

to
Mike Weaver

Acknowledgements

Acknowledgements are due to the editors of *Country Life*, the *Literary Review*, *Outposts*, *Poetry Now* (BBC), *The Poetry Book Society Anthology 1986–87*, *The Poetry Book Society Anthology 1987–88*, the *Spectator*, the *Tablet*, and of the Tate Gallery Anthology, *With a Poet's Eye*. Other poems first appeared in *21 Poems* (Celandine Press), *Kings' Children* (The Mid Northumberland Arts Group) and *Causley at 70* (Peterloo Poets).

The author acknowledges assistance from the Arts Council of Great Britain.

Boulge

Edward FitzGerald sleeps
Under this sheet of stone,
Neat as never in life,
Innocent, alone.

The earth that he lies in is his.
Grass and willow-herb drown
The wilderness path through the trees.
The great house is down.

He longed to lie in birdsound.
To be ash. To dare
The salt of the ocean and find
Lodging there.

Flint-eyed, the church, the tower
Shadow his page.
Thinly the Persian rose
Frets in its cage.

It is He that hath made us. And he
Who is lying among
Hard voices of pebble and shard
Holds his tongue.

Sibard's Well

My house, named for the Saxon spring,
Stands by the sour farmyard, the long-
Dry lip that once was Sibard's Well
Buried beneath a winding-stone
To stop the cattle falling in;
Yet underfoot is still the sound
At last of night, at first of day,
In country silences, a thin
Language of water through the clay.

At mornings, in small light, I hear
Churn-clink, the bucket handle fall.
An iron shirt, a sudden spear
Unprop themselves from the farm wall.
A voice, in a far, altered speech
Beneath my window seems to say,
'I too lived here. I too awoke
In quarter-light, when life's cold truth
Was all-too clear. As clearly spoke.'

Bridie Wiles

Bridie Wiles, 2 Gas Court Lane,
Between the tanyard and the railway line,
About the time of the first Armistice
Scooped me, one Saturday, out of my pram.
Promised me the river.

My cousin Gwennie, nine,
And three foot eight to Bridie's five eleven
Said, 'You do
And I'll chuck you in too.
Anyway,
The water isn't deep enough today
To drown a frog in.'

'Nor is it,' Bridie said, sometimes
Quite sensible despite her role
As our local madwoman
Of Chaillot,
Making to bale me
Back into the pram,
If the wrong way round.

Decades on,
At Uncle Heber's Co-op funeral,
'I'll tell you something you don't know,'
Said Gwen.
'Between us, Bridie and me pulling
As if you were a Christmas cracker
We dropped you on your head.
I never told your mum. Or mine.
My God, but you went white!
We thought that you'd gone dead.

'Another thing.
It's always been a mystery to me
How you're the only one
Of our lot doing what you do.
The other day I read
That sort of thing can be set off
By a dint on the head.
Do you think that's true?
Perhaps you owe it all to Bridie and to me.'

I asked her what she meant by it and all.
'Not possible,' said cousin Gwen, 'to say.
Though Bridie may.'

Dick Lander

When we were children at the National School
We passed each day, clipped to the corner of
Old Sion Street, Dick Lander, six foot four,
Playing a game of trains with match-boxes.

He poked them with a silver-headed cane
In the seven kinds of daily weather God
Granted the Cornish. Wore a rusted suit.
It dangled off him like he was a tree.

My friend Sid Bull, six months my senior, and
A world authority on medicine,
Explained to me just what was wrong with Dick.
'Shell-shopped,' he said. 'You catch it in the war.'

We never went too close to Dick in case
It spread like measles. 'Shell-shopped, ain't you,
    Dick?'
The brass-voiced Sid would bawl. Dick never
    spoke.
Carried on shunting as if we weren't there.

My Auntie said before he went away
Dick was a master cricketer. Could run
As fast as light. Was the town joker. Had
Every girl after him. Was spoiled quite out

Of recognition, and at twenty-one
Looked set to take the family business on
(Builders' merchants, seed, wool, manure and
    corn).
'He's never done a day's work since they sent

'Him home after the Somme,' my Uncle grinned.
'If he's mazed as a brush, my name's Lord George.
Why worry if the money's coming in?'
At firework time we throw a few at Dick.

Shout, 'Here comes Kaiser Bill!' Dick stares us
    through
As if we're glass. We yell, 'What did you do
In the Great War?' And skid into the dark.
'Choo, choo,' says Dick. 'Choo, choo, choo, choo,
    choo, choo.'

Kelly Wood

Walking in Kelly Wood, gathering words
Frail as spilt leaves, fine sticks of sentences,
Spirals of bracken from the fallen ground,
I listen for the silences of stone,
The stream's white voice, the indifference of birds.
Safe in my quiet house I lay them out
– Leaf, stick and bracken – in the hearth's cold
    frame,
Strike steel on flint against the page of dark,
Wait patiently for the first spark. A flame.

This Clock

This clock belonged to Maisie. I first heard
Its shrill tick, like the beat of a too-swift
Mineral heart, the night my mother and I
Went to the Big House for the washing. We
Sat by the kitchen range while Maisie packed
The flasket tight as a boulder, the tin clock
Pelting split seconds from the mantelshelf.

The only servant in that ugly house
With its own blackvoiced rookery, Maisie was
My mother's Friend: wire-thin, her face as pale
As a submariner's, hands rubbed so clean
The light shone through them, hard apron and cap,
Stockings field-grey and flat black shoes with
    straps.

Sharp-faced, voice barely a whisper, Maisie fought
The endless fight with all uncleanliness:
Beat hell out of the Indian carpets, turned
Parquet floors into ice-rinks, flayed stone steps
Already Whitsun-white. For dirtier dirt
She wore home-made fatigues: sackcloth apron,
Boots, a man's cap. 'Dressed like Sal Scratch,' they
    said.

She always promised me this clock that still
Fusses inside its Gothic wooden house
Of marquetry and glass. Pasted behind
The pendulum, in wilted gold on black,
The image of an eagle flying in
Delivering a field-marshal's baton
Over a muddle of trumpets, drums and flags.

Once, as a grammar schoolboy, Clever Dick,
I said to Maisie, 'If there wasn't such
A thing as dirt we'd have invented it.
What would some people do without it?' She,
Helping us out at home, my mother ill
In bed, thought this not worth replying to.
'There's not much in it, Maisie,' I said, shamed
As she came downstairs with my chamber pot.
'It makes no odds,' she said, expressionless.
'Needs emptying, a little or a lot.'

Sunday School Outing

They always say
He's fond of little children.
Liza Tremlett, lives next the church,
Punishing her front door-step
With a bass broom
Casts a laser eye
Into the God-filled sky.
A sky like coal.

It is the once-a-year day
Of the Outing
To sand and sea.
Breathless, we scale
Sam Prout's aboriginal
'Queen of Cornubia'
Parked between St Cyprian's
And the conker tree.

The vicar, camouflaged
In sea-side suit
And straw boater
Going yellow,
Reads out the roll
Checking for stowaways.
Boys in braces, knee-length
Stockings and sandals.

Girls with ribbons,
Cotton-frocks like bell-tents
With flowers on.
Pasties, Thermoses, spades,
Tin buckets, cuts of lemon
For fallible travellers.
Lightning razors
The heavy air.

They always say
He's fond of little children,
Says Liza, voice of granite.
Well, now's He's chance.
The 'Queen of Cornubia'
Lurches uneasily into the eager,
Quite unrelenting
All-day rain.

Buffalo

Buffalo Jenkyn,
Five foot by three,
Came through the First War
Scatheless. Bullets
And shrapnel bounced
Off him, they said.

Skin, hair, clothes,
All buffalo-coloured.
Wore his head low.
Chest an escarpment
In the Rockies.
He'd have braked a riot.

Worked on the road-gang.
Shoved the trolley
And electric pole
With one hand,
Pasty and bottle of tea
Trapped in the other.

Face like a volcano.
After a day digging
Holes, raising poles,
Tended his allotment.
Moved about it
Like a mass priest.

Lived bottom of
Trelawny Street
With a slat-thin whippet.
Also two shiny cats that
Trailed him as if
He were St Jerome.

Bible, Koran, Bhagavad-Gita:
The Small Gardener.
Music, the noise of things
Growing. Today was at
Church for the first
And last time.

Leaves a hole
In the universe.
I see him making
The Fiddler's Bitch at 10.29,
Cut cabbage in one hand,
In the other, violets.

Gelibolu

The path, under a thin scribble of pine,
Wavers towards a bay, a sudden shine
Of Turkish pebbles, sand, a banjo pier
Drowned in an evening sea: the scene as clear
As if painted on glass, and which would take
Only a breath, a syllable to break.

Across the strait a pharos flirts an eye.
Rough hills, smoothed to a sunset blackness, lie
Like children's cut-outs laid against the sky.
But this is savaged air. Is poisoned ground.
Unstilled, the dead, the living voices sound,
And now the night breaks open like a wound.

Seder

The room at first sight is a winter room:
The tablecloth a fresh snowfall ordered
With frail *matzot* that splinter at the touch
Like too-fine ice, the wine glasses of hard
Snow-crystal. To the shifting candle-flame,
Blood-glint of wine against the polished green
Of garlands, white of bitter herbs, and on

Its ritual dish the shankbone of the lamb.
A chair stands empty for the celebrant,
Unfree, who cannot celebrate; the wine
Poured for Elijah; the half *matzah* snugged
In a napkin for a young child to find.
The reading of the Haggadah begins.
Let those who are an hungered come and eat

With us. Those who are needy come and keep
The Passover with us. Though we dwell here
This year in exile and in bondage, next
Year we are free. Prayers in a mash of tongues.
Why does this night differ from other nights?
A boy is asked. Another at the door
Opens it that Elijah enters in

To blazon the Messiah, drink the wine
Of the unending promise, share the hope
Of Passover. Kisses, embraces as
The feast is ended. We disperse beneath
Uncounted stars as measureless as those
Children who marched into the wilderness.
Laughter. *Yom Tov. A Good Yom Tov*, they say,

This family, sometime traders in salt
In Novgorod: doctor, attorney, truck-
Driver, schoolteacher, mail-clerk, student, nurse;
The smiling grandparents, from whom God hid
His face, their eyes in shadow from the harsh
Rumour of yesterday. Every one
A trader still in necessary salt.

A Little Story

Taking, at last, the heart's advice
He walked towards the morning sea,
Felt its salt promise on his tongue,
For the first time in years was free.

The sun came up a richer red.
He saw it swallow up the dew;
Laughed as the white incredible stars
Still wavered in the risen blue.

To his surprise, the one he left
Declared an addled life and wrung
Desperate hands (so he was told)
And threatened self-destruction.

Indifferent, he journeyed on;
Tasted new wine and newer bread.
Tilled his own garden. Said, I feel
Somehow new-risen from the dead.

Reaching a tender fame, he seemed
As self-sufficient as the sun.
Safe in a tower of words he hid
His gradual wound from all but one

Who found, unsought, another love;
Untaught, another life to live,
While he who listened to the heart
Pondered on the alternative:

Bugis Street

Over our heads long skeins of light
Fly Bugis Street, each lamp a white
Bulging eyeball. We sit out on
The buckled strip of hosed-down stone
Silted with chairs and tables; stare
Like children at a country fair
That smells of sea-damp, joss-sticks, drains.

Music discharges like a gun.
I drink a Tiger beer. You take
A coffee laced with ginger; make
No comment as the girls parade
In polished gowns, spangles, gilt shoes,
Ear-rings as long as icicles
And scalloped wigs in dangerous shades

Of lollipop. On each slant face
The necessary mask of pure
Defiance; a sharp mouth that trades
The ritual obscenities
With those who pass unseeing; dare
To mock the solemn ordinance,
The painted glance that fails to hide,

Somehow, a terrible innocence.
Peddlers flicker among the crowd
With cassettes, T-shirts, watches, loud
Pictures in silk of matadors;
And for a dollar Singapore
Photographs of the girls. But they
Are boys. The stars are glass. The sea

A cauldron of voices. The moon's ray
A searchlight crawling on the bay.
We leave. A peddler blocks our path;
Reads every word I do not say,
Pushes an orchid dunked in gold
Across the dirty tablecloth
And my hand shakes, but not with cold.

In Malacca

I saw St Francis Xavier today
As I went through the Santiago Gate:
Stone-faced, stone-frocked, fisherman's arms apart
As if to show the one that got away
To the slow farmer with the bullock cart,
The sailboat crossing, re-crossing the strait,
The dredger swallowing the level bay.

On ticket of leave from the Arts Festival
(Doing Malaysia in half a day)
I plant the page with words; attempt a print
Of gilt-voiced temples, a brown waterfall,
The elephant-headed god in Goldsmith Street
– Four-handed, mover of obstacles – intent
On smiling sleep, a rat across his feet.

Safe in their trope of forest leaves a pair
Of spider-monkeys sip the critical air
Where softly in the paper jungle wait
The patient tiger and the five-step snake.

Arshile Gorky's The Artist and His Mother

They face us as if we were marksmen, eyes
Unblindfolded, quite without pathos, lives
Fragile as the rose-coloured light, as motes
Of winking Anatolian dust. But in
The landscape of the mind they stand as strong
As rock or water.
                The young boy with smudged
Annunciatory flowers tilts his head
A little sideways like a curious bird.
He wears, against his history's coming cold
A velvet-collared coat, Armenian pants,
A pair of snub-nosed slippers. He is eight
Years old. His mother, hooded as a nun,
Rests shapeless, painted hands; her pinafore
A blank white canvas falling to the floor.

Locked in soft shapes of ochre, iron, peach,
Burnt gold of dandelion, their deep gaze
Is unaccusing, yet accusatory.
It is as if the child already sees
His dead mother beside him as they fled
Barefoot to starving Yerevan. And sees
His own death, self-invited, in the green
Of a new world, the painted visions now
Irrelevant, and arguments of line
Stilled by the death of love.

                              Abandoning
His miracle, he makes the last, long choice
Of one who can no longer stay to hear
Promises of the eye, the colour's voice.

I believe you were born in Odessa

Never having heard
The splash of a syllable
Or read as much as a comma
By my Russian friend,
I said as we walked
By the shaken fabric
Of a black sea,
'I believe you were born in Odessa.
Did you never see Chekhov?'

Squaring off his pince-nez
He replied, 'My mother once glimpsed
The back of him. A tall man
In a white linen suit,
White linen hat,
And carrying a cane.
Climbing the steps
Of a sea-front hotel.'

'Did he not say this?' I said.
 ' "It is very hard
 To describe the sea.
 But once I read
 What a schoolboy wrote.
 The sea is huge.
 Just that. No more.
 I think that is beautiful." '

Glancing at the silver egg
That was his watch,
'Time to return
To the Literature Conference,'
My friend remarked. A tall man
In a white linen suit,
White linen hat,
And carrying a cane.
Climbing the steps
Of a sea-front hotel.

On the Eastern Front

To Helmut Pabst

He lies locked in a wood of winter snow.
The snow is blue, the shadows indigo.
If he could speak, I would not understand.
Ice seals the rifle to his silent hand.

A burst of snowflakes slithers from a fir,
Blunting the soldier's sight. He does not stir,
Nor does he speak, though what he says is clear
As the glass sky, the unforgiving air.

A Song of Truth

When Christ the Lord of Heaven was born
Cold was the land.
His mother saw along the road
A fig-tree stand.
'Good Mary, leave the figs to grow
For we have thirty miles to go.
The hour is late.'

Mary came near unto the town.
Stayed at a door.
Said to the little farmer, 'Pray
Let us stay here.
Not for myself these words I make
But for an infant child's sake.
The night is chill.'

The farmer opened up his barn.
Bade them go in.
When half the winter night had gone
Came there again.
'Where you are from in this wide world,
And are not killed by winter cold,
I cannot tell.'

The farmer came into his house
The barn beside.
'Rise up, dear wife,' he cried, 'and may
Best fire be made
That these poor travellers are warm
And safe from wind and weather's harm
Here at our hearth.'

Smiling, Mary then entered in
The farmhouse door;
Also her good and gentle man
That self-same hour
Drew from his pack a crock of tin,
With snow the young child filled it fine,
And it was flour.

Crystals of ice he placed therein
As sugar rare
And water that white milk should be
Both fresh and fair.
Over the flame they hung the crock,
And such soft sweetness did they cook,
Was finest pap.

Of wooden chip the good man carved
With homely blade
A spoon that was of ivory
And diamond made.
And now the child does Mary sweet
Give of the pap that He may eat:
Jesus his name.

translated from the German

In the Dome Car

The train, as if departure were a state-
Secret, pulls out without a sound. I glance
Up from *The Globe and Mail* surprised to see
Through the dome car's dull window, Canada
Lurching quietly by. *Find the dome car,*
You said to me. *You'll see it all from there.*

And so I do. Or think I do. At first,
The Bow River, surface of china blue,
Indigo-coloured water squeezing through;
The rail-cars straightening in line ahead.
Giacometti trees like naked men
Stand, sky-high, in a littleness of snow;
Adverts for Honda, holidays (*Try us
Ski Jasper*); hunks of rock; the red Dutch barn
Recurring like a decimal; a thin
Smear of gold-leaf that is the coming corn.

In ice-edged light the train moves cautiously
Above a toy village, a clip of black
And white Indian ponies, a tepee
Hoisted beside a brake of pointed sticks.
A bridge hurries to meet us; spills across
A frozen lake. A car parked on the ice,
In shifting light, glitters a mile from shore.
We gape at it. But what I see is you
Walking the long nave of the train-station,
Never turning. *You'll see it all from there.*

We rush the stone horizon. At the last
Moment the mountains part; admit us to
Indian country, where the patient snow
Refuses the year's passage, scars the floor
Of a pale valley; lies in wait for more.

A Tamarack Goose

Observe this decoy goose made by
The Woodland Cree
Of scented bentwood broken
From the tamarack tree.

Two little shocks of larch
Make a hollow head
Clinched at the beak
With a tense delicacy of thread.

The body a delicious
Plumpness of twigs;
Neatly pollarded squab tail.
It stands on three legs.

A nothingness of mask and eye
Against the spring snows
Mimics the white cheek patch
Of the Canada goose.

When, at Epiphany,
I opened its gold box
There rose a fragrance
Of musk and sacred forest sticks.

I took the gift as a sign
Of trust, fidelity.
Hold on, have faith,
It seemed to say.

And so we did until the thin
Bond between us broke;
Neither having seen in the decoy goose
The joke.

At the Château Lake Louise

There was no need of snow
To chill the valley's bone;
There was no need of ice
To wrap the naked stone.

Stilled by each other's blood
Silent, at last, we lay;
Watched as the winter sun
Rode down the day.

Nothing was said; no glance
Traded of ice or fire;
No shaft, it seemed, wounded
The usual air

As each, with civil care
And words unspoken, thought
In separate silences
To unbruise the heart.

So we may never know,
Betrayer and betrayed,
In this small history
Which part was played.

Voiceless, the mountain smokes
Above the glacier wall,
Stubble of pine and fir,
The rigid waterfall.

Colours of lake and sky
Pale in lost light;
Ebb to simplicities
Of black, of white.

Myth

And the children, brother, sister,
From the mountainside returning

Saw at last their camp discovered
By the Morning Star Man. Saw him

Kill the cattle. Kill the people.
Kill the father. Kill the mother.

All the lovely people murdered.
For a while they sat among them

Their small words of comfort speaking
That the dead might hear their voices

As when living breath was with them.
The two children, sister, brother,

Seizing up a firestick journeyed
Over the red plain, the mountain

And the ever-swimming river
To the rim of a tall forest

And among the fern and flower
By a spring of silver water

Built a campfire, sat them down there;
Watched the sun bloody the ocean,

And above their heads a starshine
Printed in another fashion.

Suns and moons flew by like fireflies
As they lived alone, together.

'I want you as wife,' the boy said.
Said the girl, 'You are my brother.'

'We are as the forest creatures,'
Said the boy. 'Or those that wander

'The red plain. As free birds flying
The high blue. As fish that journey

'The long silences of water.
You shall be my wife,' the boy said.

And the sister and the brother
Lay and made a child together.

Made them children as the seasons
Flowed about them like a river.

And the children, men and women,
Wandering to nameless countries,

Made a speech from leaf and flower,
Made from ice and snow another,

Made a speech from mist and mountain,
From the sands a speech of fire.

'I have lost my spear for hunting,'
Said the brother. 'And must find it.'

Back they journeyed to the campground
By the spring of silver water.

Many men and many women
Walked that ground. And she was calling,

'Here your hunting spear is lying
Where we two first lay together.'

And the man came to the woman,
On her lips placed a soft finger.

'Speak,' he said. 'And I must kill you.
As the Morning Star Man. Kill you.'

Laid his cutting-stone beside her.

Samuel Palmer's Coming from Evening Church

The heaven-reflecting, usual moon
Scarred by thin branches, flows between
The simple sky, its light half-gone,
The evening hills of risen green.
Safely below the mountain crest
A little clench of sheep holds fast.
The lean spire hovers like a mast
Over its hulk of leaves and moss
And those who, locked within a dream,
Make between church and cot their way
Beside the secret-springing stream
That turns towards an unknown sea;
And there is neither night nor day,
Sorrow nor pain, eternally.

St Godric and the Hart

Out of the river clear
The silver hart has sprung
The dike of thorn and briar
To where the holy man
In breast-plate and rough gown
At his house of small stone
Attends in northern air
The Virgin and her song.

Here in the turning wood
He builds himself a sure
Lodging of prayer and psalm
Where country creatures share
His wood-fire and his fare
Against season and storm,
And here the hart may bear
Its crown of spines, of blood.

Startled of head and eye
The hart on a green path
Pauses for its torn breath,
The hunting pack, the horn
Sounding along the shore
As the Saint stands alone,
Bids the hart hide its cry
And enter at his door.

Calm in his ragged shawl
He waits, perfect in faith,
By stirring bush and tree,
Huntsman and brawling hound
Ringing the bright grove round.
'Father!' the hunters call.
'Tell with God's tongue of truth
Where may our quarry be?'

'God knows,' he says, he smiles;
The hunters too, as they
Spur onwards for the kill,
And with their quarry he
Keeps quiet house until
The hart, at even-fall,
To the world's wood runs free:
As, pleasing God, may we.

The Prodigal Son

I could remember nothing of the village:
Only, at a sharp elbow in the lane
Between the train-station and the first cottage,
An August cornfield flowing down to meet me;
At its dry rim a spatter of scarlet poppies.

I had forgotten the cement-botched church,
The three spoilt bells my grandmother had
      christened
Crock, Kettle and Pan; the cider-sharp Devon
      voices,
The War Memorial with my uncle's name
Spelt wrongly, women in working black, black
      stockings,
White aprons, sober washing lines, my Bramley-
Cheeked aunt picking blackberries in her cap,
The butcher's cart, the baker's cart from Chudleigh,
From Christow, and the hard-lipped granite quarry
Coughing up regular dust under the skyline.

But this came later. I heard as I climbed
The white flint lane the still-insistent voices.
'Never go back,' they said. 'Never go back.'
This was before the fall of corn, the poppies.

Out of the sun's dazzle, somebody spoke my name.

Legend of the Raven

Raven, hill-scavenging, was first to see
The cave fill with bold light, the farmers turn
From lambing to stare skyward as a burn
Of swift stars broke on winter field and tree.

Dog-fox, becalmed, lay at the pasture brink.
The herdsman, stick upraised, stood stiff as rock
Watching from the Long Meadow where the flock
Bent to the halted stream, but did not drink.

Wanting of fire and food under the hill
The shepherds gazed into the wheeling blue,
Hands reaching to the crock suddenly still.

The golden cloud about the cave withdrew.
Raven, now squinting from the mountain-crest
Saw where a young child took his mother's breast.

Embryos

i

Emily Dickinson
Called last night.
You are a poor cook,
She said. And look,
These windows
Need cleaning.
As for your poems,
Listen to me
A moment.

ii

When I was sent at 10
To order a bag
Of coal (2/-),
Mr Fairbrother
Showed me the two saucer
Shapes he had made
In the floor
Standing at the same
Desk for 57 years
(Less the First War).
He wore them like
Medals.

iii

Don't seem to dream
So much these days
About being Jackie Coogan,
My life as
Alexander the Great, or
The bulkhead imploding
In the Bay and the water
Spirting in. More often
I'm at the back of the Mixed
Infants, aged fifty-two,
The only one who can't
Get past G in
The alphabet.

Letter to W.S. Graham

Dear Sydney, or
Should I call
You Willie,
I don't know

Which. We only
Met once and
Didn't call each
Other anything.

Sitting here in
The thick bit
Of Cornwall
Watching the day

Move round my
Two cypress trees
I was thinking of
You and Nessie down

At the sharp end,
Enduring as usual
The first bite of
The Atlantic. I

Heard you were
Ill and hope
You're bettering.
One thing, your

Poetry was never
Under that sort
Of weather. I
Turn to it as to

A spring that has
Not failed me in
Forty years. In
Your fishbone

Tweed, silk
Stock and glass
Shoes you looked
To me like a

1st War Colonel
(Ret.) and not
The Wild Man
Of Madron I'd

Been warned to
Expect. But like
All poets, you were
In disguise; a

Good one, too;
Though when you
Said a few
Words on my

Behalf from the
Dead body
Of the Hall at
That reading I

Feared you might
Say something
Awful. Like. Or.
But it was O.

K. I thank you;
Think of you as
The Genuine Miracle
Working Icon

Man wandering
Starved and wind-
Scraped Zennor
Where the cows

If not the
Poets ate the
Bell-ropes.
The day I

Called with the
Fan from Germany
There was no reply
To doortaps and

You weren't in
The pub either.
Maybe you were
There all the

Time and took no
Notice. If so,
Fine. Noticing should
Be put to better

Uses. So continue
Listening for
The sound the land
Makes, the signals

The ocean sends, the
Secret speeches of
Air and fire as
You move about the

Scrubbed bracken,
The simple strong
Flowers, the written
And unwritten stones,

In the long fret of
The sea. You will always
Be there for me, always
Standing at the gate

Of Madron Black
Wood, a salt
Poem in your ever
Greenock hand.

I love the laurel green

After Etienne Jodelle

I love the laurel green, whose verdant flame
Burns its bright victory on the winter day,
Calls to eternity its happy name
And neither time nor death shall wear away.

I love the holly tree with branches keen,
Each leaflet fringed with daggers sharp and small.
I love the ivy, too, winding its green,
Its ardent stem about the oak, the wall.

I love these three, whose living green and true
Is as unfailing as my love for you
Always by night and day whom I adore.

Yet the green wound that stays within me more
Is ever greener than these three shall be:
Laurel and ivy and the holly tree.

Calico

Calico, ledged on the calico mountain,
Lodges in an empty pocket of silver
Over the sand-drenched plain, the Mojave
Forging its secret journey under
Sidewinder spiralling, sidewinder rattling,
Dusky heronsbill, desert-tea,
Flowering beavertail cactus, the sharpened
Bible spears of the Joshua tree.

Fresher than paint, the ghost of a ghost town
Takes its stand in the twelve-o'clock light:
Parking Lot, Ice Cream Parlor, Playhouse,
Schoolhouse dribbling the stars and stripes,
Repro guns and saddles and stetsons,
Rock shop, bottle shop, needlepoint store,
C & H Smelter, bath house, jail house,
Lil's Saloon and the Maggie Mine Tour.
Shadowless, the shadows wander
Broken adobe wall and stair.
Out of the canyon the poor-will startles
Like a bell the immaculate air.

And the Cornish were here, their names like
    granite
Scoured by a century of sun,
The vanished voices hymning to Zion,
Hollowed out by the accents of home.
I see Wheal Abraham, dark King Doniert's
Stone (which he raised for the good of his soul),
Tide-water sidling into Newlyn,
The weathercock swirling its gold on Paul.

The Mystery of St Mylor

Dateless, quite weightless, the Holy Boy
Hovers alone in frosty light,
His naked tomb fringed with the gold
Of winter furze and aconite.

His silver hand, his brazen foot
Are fire against a sky of slate
And now are flesh and bone, and by
A miracle, articulate.

Here it was the virgin earth
Opened her side where he might lie,
Drew a green field above his brow
Until his huntsman passed him by.

And neither fell the rain nor hail,
Nor ever spear of grass has grown,
And never a rag of snow that lay
Upon this roofless box of stone.

But when beside the famished sea
Prince Mylor lay as on a bed,
Silently his assassin came
And severed him his glittering head.

Plant your broad staff, Prince Mylor cried,
*And it shall branch and it shall blow
And at its foot a root shall spring
And from that root a stream shall flow.*

Tell me, I asked the Holy Boy,
The true mystery that you spell.
I leaned and listened for his voice.
It was the ringing of a bell.

At St Hilary

Between two Cornish seas, the spire
Blazes the land, the waving air.

The dark stem of a Celtic cross
Sprouts, half-grown, from the shallow grass.

A tomb, exploded, shows the bones
Of a young sycamore. Slant stones

Cram the graveyard like ships stormbound.
A wasted urn drips shard and sand.

Like auguries, two seabirds lie
Motionless in the squalling sky.

Through rain and wind and risen snow
I come, as fifty years ago,

Drawn by I know not what, to sound
A fabled shore, unlost, unfound,

Where in the shadow of the sun
Past, present, future, wait as one.

Only the breathing ash speaks true.
Nothing is new. Nothing is new

As the sea slinks to where I stand
Between the water and the land.

St Protus & St Hyacinth, Blisland

The church, a stack of granite harvested
From Bodmin Moor, glints through uncovered trees
Above a valley loud with water, rocks,
Voices of bald-faced rooks that lurk and strut
High shelves of ash and sycamore. Beside

The porch the tilted ground is lit
With primrose, sharp-eyed daisy, daffodil,
The castor-oil plant gleams within a frame
Of window-stone, pure Georgian glass. Inside,
Along the nave, rough trunks of granite lean

Time-pressed this way, that way, in greying light.
Christ dies a gold death on the painted screen.
The altar glitters like a carousel.
The gilt tears of the Maries shine and fall.
Outside, a sudden pagan breeze, snow cool,

Flows from the waste of quoits and circled stones,
Roughens the grass skin of the goose-green where
Children shrill on the gibbet of a swing.
A boy in studded shirt and helmet revs
His bike up, circles endlessly the green

As though, for him, the day will never end.
Dark! Dark! the rooks warn. *Soon it will be dark!*
Unseen, an aircraft breaks the Cornish sky.
The two saints shudder on their granite plinth.
Pray for us, says Protus, says Hyacinth.

Trethevy Quoit

Sea to the north, the south.
At the moor's crown
Thin field, hard-won, turns on
The puzzle of stones.
Lying in dreamtime here
Knees dragged to chin,
With dagger, food and drink –
Who was that one?
      None shall know, says bully blackbird.
      None.

Field threaded with flowers
Cools in lost sun.
Under furze bank, yarrow
Sinks the drowned mine.
By spoil dump and bothy
Down the moor spine
Hear long-vanished voices
Falling again.
      Now they are all gone, says bully blackbird.
      All gone.

Hedgebirds loose on wild air
Their dole of song.
From churchtown the tractor
Stammers. Is dumb.
In the wilderness house
Of granite, thorn,
Ask where are those who came.
Ask why we come.
      Home, says bully blackbird.
      Where is home?

Red

Scrabbling for words, 'Don't do a thing,' I said,
'I wouldn't do.' And in that second, knew
From the lost look you gave, turning away,
We'd never meet again. Twenty years on,
The detail of your face is gone. I see
Only the coil of Easter flowers that lay
Crowning the moist hedge just above your head.
I saw the flowers there again today.

In storms, you were the rock we rested on,
Gave to the hopeless hope, tempered the mad,
Kept the worn faith when things were worse than
    bad;
Cast in the role of calm, consoling one
Persuaded us, because it was unspoken,
That ties of love, of blood could not be broken
And healed our loss, but never told your own
Until the day you journeyed off alone,
Checked in at some hotel, climbed the roof-stair,
Fell, with your secret, on the assenting air.

My Enemy

My enemy was the pork butcher's son.
I see him, head and shoulders over me,
Sphinx-faced, his cheeks the colour of lard, the eyes
Revolver-blue through Bunter spectacles.
When we lined up for five to nine at school
He'd get behind me, crumple up a fist,
Stone thumb between the first and second fingers;
Punch out a tune across my harp of ribs.

Ten years ahead of Chamberlain, I tried
Appeasement, with the same results: gave him
My lunch of bread and cheese, the Friday bun,
The Lucky Bags we bought at Maggie Snell's.
One Armistice I wept through the Two Minutes
Because my dad was killed in France (not true).
'Poor little sod, his father's dead,' my enemy
Observed, discreetly thumping me again.

I took the scholarship exam not for
The promise of Latin, Greek, but to escape
My enemy. The pork butcher's sharp son
Passed too, and I remember how my heart
Fell like a bucket down a summer well
The day Boss Ward read out our names. And how,
Quite unaccountably, the torment stopped
Once we were at the Grammar. We've not met

Since 1939, although I heard
How as a gunner in the long retreat
Hauling the piece from Burma, he was met
At the first village by naked kids with stones,
Placards reading 'Quit India.' After that,
Nothing; except our pair of sentences
To thirty years in chalk Siberias:
Which one of us is which hard to define
For children in the butcher's class, and mine.

When I Was 14

After the workhouse concert, the stone hall
A mix of Lysol and washed slate, the boys
In penitential boots and jerseys, girls
In stubborn aprons, eyes of men and women
The eyes of those in a defeated country,
They brought their Singing Man to entertain us.
'To thank the artistes,' said the Workhouse Master.

The Singing Man, bald as a pebble, fringe
Of stiff pale hair about the jaw, arranged
One hand from cheek to ear, drew a white bead
On the roof-beam; faltered a drift of song.
His fellows gazed at him, at us, delighted
At such madness, as we were too (though with
More circumspection). And the singer, grown

Too-conscious, suddenly, of his wandering song
Pointed a judge's finger at himself,
Retreated, grinning, to our kind applause:
The song unended he had brought from field
And folk of childhood. All I now recall
Is richness offered in return for dross,
The memory of a certain wound, a song lost.

Family Feeling

My Uncle Alfred had the terrible temper.
Wrapped himself up in its invisible cloak.
When the mood was on his children crept from the kitchen.
It might have been mined. Not even the budgie spoke.

He was killed in the First World War in Mesopotamia.
His widow rejoiced, though she never wished him dead.
After three years a postcard arrived from Southampton.
'Coming home Tuesday. Alf,' was what it said.

His favourite flower he called the antimirrhinum.
Grew it instead of greens on the garden plot.
Didn't care much for children, though father of seven.
Owned in his lifetime nine dogs all called Spot.

At Carnival time he rode the milkman's pony.
Son of the Sheikh, a rifle across his knee.
Alf the joiner as Peary in cotton-wool snowstorms.
Secret in cocoa and feathers, an Indian Cree.

I recognized him once as the Shah of Persia.
My auntie's front-room curtains gave him away.
'It's Uncle Alf!' I said, but his glance was granite.
'Mind your own business, nosey,' I heard him say.

I never knew just what it was that bugged him,
Or what kind of love a father's love could be.
One by one the children baled out of the
    homestead.
'You were too young when yours died,' they
    explained to me.

Today, walking through St Cyprian's Church-yard
I saw where he lay in a box the dry colour of bone.
The grass was tamed and trimmed as if for a
    Sunday.
Seven antimirrhinums in a jar of stone.

In 1933

I see the deep November street,
The crowd suddenly still beneath
The dark lurch of the Castle Keep
As though the evening held its breath
Before the bell-man's starting cry
And the first rocket hit the sky.

It was a children's land: a tower,
Ships, houses grumbling in low gear,
The stick-man stalking through the Square,
Paraffin torches slopping fire,
A child's heart too afraid to ask
Which was a face and which a mask.

I see the gold set-piece that read
'God Save Our Empire', as each head
In fireworks of the King and Queen
At the far end of Castle Green
Dribbled blue flame, began to sprout
Flowers of dark. Went slowly out.

Eden Rock

They are waiting for me somewhere beyond Eden
  Rock:
My father, twenty-five, in the same suit
Of Genuine Irish Tweed, his terrier Jack
Still two years old and trembling at his feet.

My mother, twenty-three, in a sprigged dress
Drawn at the waist, ribbon in her straw hat,
Has spread the stiff white cloth over the grass.
Her hair, the colour of wheat, takes on the light.

She pours tea from a Thermos, the milk straight
From an old H.P. sauce-bottle, a screw
Of paper for a cork; slowly sets out
The same three plates, the tin cups painted blue.

The sky whitens as if lit by three suns.
My mother shades her eyes and looks my way
Over the drifted stream. My father spins
A stone along the water. Leisurely,

They beckon to me from the other bank.
I hear them call, 'See where the stream-path is!
Crossing is not as hard as you might think.'

I had not thought that it would be like this.

Note

p. 14   'Gelibolu' is the Turkish name for Gallipoli.

p. 26   'A Song of Truth' (*'Ein Wahrheitslied'*) was published for the first time in *Des Knaben Wunderhorn* (1806–8), in which a number of the ballads were written by the editors themselves, Clemens Brentano and Achim von Arnim.

p. 33   The principal source of 'Myth' is Roland Robinson's *Aboriginal Myths and Legends* (Sun Books, Melbourne, 1966).

Index of titles

Arshile Gorky's *The Artist and His Mother*	21
At St Hilary	51
At the Château Lake Louise	31
Boulge	1
Bridie Wiles	3
Buffalo	12
Bugis Street	18
Calico	48
Dick Lander	5
Eden Rock	62
Embryos	41
Family Feeling	59
Gelibolu	14
I believe you were born in Odessa	23
I love the laurel green	47
In Malacca	20
In 1933	61
In the Dome Car	28
Kelly Wood	7
Legend of the Raven	40
Letter to W. S. Graham	43
Little Story, A	17
My Enemy	56
Mystery of St Mylor, The	49
Myth	33
On the Eastern Front	25
Prodigal Son, The	39
Red	55
St Godric and the Hart	37
St Protus & St Hyacinth, Blisland	52

Samuel Palmer's *Coming from Evening Church*	36
Seder	15
Sibard's Well	2
Song of Truth, A	26
Sunday School Outing	10
Tamarack Goose, A	30
This Clock	8
Trethevy Quoit	53
When I Was 14	58

Index of first lines

After the workhouse concert, the stone hall	58
And the children, brother, sister,	33
Bridie Wiles, 2 Gas Court Lane,	3
Between two Cornish seas, the spire	51
Buffalo Jenkyn,	12
Calico, ledged on the calico mountain,	48
Dateless, quite weightless, the Holy Boy	49
Dear Sydney, or	43
Edward FitzGerald sleeps	1
Emily Dickinson	41
He lies locked in a wood of winter snow.	25
I could remember nothing of the village:	39
I love the laurel green, whose verdant flame	47
I saw St Francis Xavier today	20
I see the deep November street,	61
My enemy was the pork butcher's son.	56
My house, named for the Saxon spring,	2
My Uncle Alfred had the terrible temper.	59
Never having heard	23
Observe this decoy goose made by	30
Out of the river clear	37
Over our heads long skeins of light	18
Raven, hill-scavenging, was first to see	40
Scrabbling for words, 'Don't do a thing,' I said,	55
Sea to the north, the south.	53
Taking, at last, the heart's advice	17
The church, a stack of granite harvested	52
The heaven-reflecting, usual moon	36
The path, under a thin scribble of pine,	14
There was no need of snow	31

The room at first sight is a winter room:	15
The train, as if departure were a state-	28
They always say	10
They are waiting for me somewhere beyond Eden Rock:	62
They face us as if we were marksmen, eyes	21
This clock belonged to Maisie. I first heard	8
Walking in Kelly Wood, gathering words	7
When Christ the Lord of Heaven was born	26
When we were children at the National School	5